STANDARD
LOAN

UNLESS RECALLED BY ANOTHER READER
THIS ITEM MAY BE BORROWED FOR

FOUR WEEKS

To renew, telephone:
01243 816089 (Bishop Otter)
01243 816099 (Bognor Regis)

0 4 SEP 2000

23. OCT 00

09. MAY 01.

25. FEB 06.

09. MAR 07.

1 7 FEB 2010

D1376351

Stories linking with the History
National Curriculum Key Stage 2.

First published in 1998 by Franklin Watts

This paperback edition published in 1999

Franklin Watts
96 Leonard Street
London EC2A 4RH

Franklin Watts Australia
14 Mars Road
Lane Cove
NSW 2066

Editor: Matthew Parselle
Series editor: Paula Borton
Designer: Kirstie Billingham
Consultant: Dr Anne Millard, BA Hons, Dip Ed, PhD

A CIP catalogue record for this book
is available from the British Library.

ISBN   0 7496 3457 X (pbk)
       0 7496 3089 2 (hbk)

Dewey Classification 942.01

Printed in Great Britain

Viking Raiders

by
Karen Wallace

Illustrations by Richard Morgan

W
FRANKLIN WATTS
NEW YORK • LONDON • SYDNEY

1

A Terrible Accident

Edmund pulled his tattered woollen hood over his head and leant into the wind and rain. Across a field of swaying marsh grass, he saw a low stone wall, half hidden in a clump of scraggy trees.

He turned to the huddled figure of his

sister behind him. "We'll stop there," he
shouted. But the wind ripped his voice
from his mouth and blew it across the
marsh and out to the sea beyond.

Leoba looked up. Her round face was
grey with cold. She had never felt so tired
and hungry and miserable. She couldn't
hear what her brother said but she
understood and nodded dumbly.

Edmund plodded on in front trying to shield his sister from the worst of the storm. For a week now, ever since the accident, they had been travelling on their own. And for the first time in his life, Edmund had realized how difficult it was just to survive.

In his mind's eye, Edmund pictured their destination. Five miles along the coast, their aunt and uncle lived in a settlement protected by a wooden fence.

They were kind people and since they had no children of their own, Edmund prayed they would give him and Leoba shelter.

It was even possible that news of the accident had reached the settlement.

Edmund clenched his teeth. He would never forget the *crack* as the wooden bridge had broken just as his mother, father and youngest sister were crossing the river. He would never forget how they had tumbled like dolls into the swirling muddy water below.

It was only chance that he and Leoba had lagged behind. Leoba had an eye for ripe berries. She had seen hundreds in a clump of blackberry bushes and her mother had agreed to let her pick them if Edmund stayed with her.

And so their parents had gone on ahead pushing the cart heaped with their belongings,

Emma perched on top.

Edmund had climbed up the rocky sides
of the river and had just sat down when he
saw the bridge break in half. Seconds later,
Leoba had scrambled up beside him. Her
mouth was stained with berry juice and
her brown eyes were shining.

Edmund felt a terrible lump rise in his
throat. He turned to his sister.

How could he tell her?

Then he saw Leoba's smile disappear and her face turn the colour of stone. She was staring, frozen like a statue, at the shattered planks and torn ropes swinging over the water.

Edmund watched as her skirt fell open and the precious load of blackberries tipped all over the rocks.

The wind was dropping now. Edmund wiped rain from his eyes and looked out over the marsh grass. The low stone wall was getting nearer.

Leoba spoke for the first time that day.

"Can we sleep there?"

"Of course," replied Edmund in a reassuring voice. But a nagging worry tugged at the edges of his mind. There was

something strange about the place.
Edmund shook the worry away and
walked faster. At least it was shelter.
Besides, he thought grimly, what worse
could happen to them, now?

Twenty minutes later, they followed a
twisty path into the clump of scraggy trees.
Around them the grass was trampled flat
as if by many feet. But there was no sound
of animals or men's voices.

Edmund's heart began to thud in his
chest. He remembered his father talking of
raiders who came from the north. They
landed their fast boats right up the beach.
Then they destroyed and looted everything
in their path.

Edmund looked once more at the
trampled grass. He turned and grabbed
Leoba roughly by the arm. "Something's
wrong," he said in a low hoarse voice.

"Let's get out of –"

At that moment, Leoba's face went white and she began to scream.

Edmund spun round and found himself staring face to face at four huge warriors.

They wore dull metal helmets, some with strips over the nose and eyes. Their beards were blonde and red, thick and matted. They held wooden shields and long sharp spears.

Behind him Leoba screamed again and began to run.

The tallest one pulled back his spear arm and aimed straight at Leoba's back.

"Don't kill her!" yelled Edmund. He tried to run but his arms were held in a grip of iron. In front of him, Leoba stumbled and fell. He heard a sharp *thud* as her head hit something hard on the ground. Then she lay still.

2

An Unknown Fate

Leoba opened her eyes and looked around
her. It was dark and the room was going
up and down, up and down. Outside
she heard the slurp and crash of water
on wood.

Panic seized her. She was on a boat.

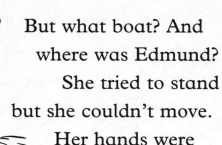

But what boat? And where was Edmund? She tried to stand but she couldn't move. Her hands were chained! The panic exploded into terror and a choked scream escaped from her mouth.

Something moved beside her.

"Leoba! It's me, Edmund!"

In the murky darkness, Leoba felt Edmund's skinny arm around her. "You're all right! I'm so glad you're all right!"

Leoba fought the sobs that shook her whole body. "Where are we, Edmund? How did we get here?" A sob stuck in her throat. "Why are we chained?"

"We are captives," said Edmund in a low voice. "Those warriors were Vikings. This is their ship."

Leoba shook her head as if she was trying to remember something. "I, I – ," she began.

"You fell and hit your head," said Edmund gently. "You've been unconscious for two days." He shrugged. "At least I think it's two days. It's difficult to tell down here."

"But where are they taking us?" asked Leoba. "How are we going to get home?"

"Home?" said Edmund bitterly. "What home? Have you forgotten that, too?"

Leoba put her hands over her face.

In the darkness, Edmund patted her arm. "I'm sorry," he whispered. "I didn't mean to be unkind."

Leoba laid her hand on his. "I know."

"We are being taken to a town called Hedeby," said Edmund in a stronger voice. "It is a trading town. Merchants come to sell silks and spices, and buy furs and walrus tusks to take back to their own countries."

"How do you know this?"

"The sailor who has been bringing us food and water told me," replied Edmund. "He is called Olaf and is kind enough."

The mention of food made Leoba realize she was very hungry indeed.

As if he had read her mind, Edmund fished into a pouch tied to his belt. He handed her a piece of bread and some dried meat. "I've kept you some every day," he said. "Just in case you woke up."

Leoba bit into the hard sour bread.
It tasted disgusting and faintly fishy but it
was food.

"Where is this town called Hedeby? Is it in
our country?" she asked.

Edmund shook his head. "It is in a
place called Jutland. "We arrive on the
morning tide. Olaf will come for us."

"And the other warriors, the ones I saw," said Leoba, shaking as she spoke. "Are they on this ship?"

Edmund nodded. "Their leader is the captain. He is the red beard who ordered your capture. His name is Harald but I have not seen him since we were taken below."

They sat in silence for a moment.

"At least we are together," said Leoba. She swallowed. "And perhaps we will find a way home, after all."

"Perhaps we will," said Edmund in as firm a voice as he could manage. But to himself he was saying something completely different.

Edmund was sure he and Leoba would never see their own country again.

3

A Strange Land

"Wake up," growled a deep voice. "We are in Hedeby. The captain wants you."

Edmund sat up with a jerk.

The sailor Olaf was pushing bread and a horn of watery ale into his hand.

"What is going to be happen to us?"

A pained look passed over Olaf's broad whiskery face.

"I – I believe you will be staying in this town for several days," he said gruffly. "After that I know not."

Ten minutes later Edmund and Leoba were standing on deck.

At first they could only blink and stare
around them. They were in the middle
of a huge long ship shaped like a willow
leaf. Both ends swept high out of the
water. The front was carved into the
head of a fierce dragon, its lips pulled
back to show sharp gold teeth and a
scarlet forked tongue.

Out of the corner of her eye, Leoba
saw the red-
bearded warrior
whose face
was the last
thing she
remembered
before
passing out.
So this was
Captain Harald. She
drew in a sharp breath.

Captain Harald sat on a sea chest picking his teeth with the point of a small dagger.

As they came closer, he smiled wolfishly. He had the palest of blue eyes and long lines etched into his weathered high-boned face.

The children stopped in front of him.

He put his heavy hands on Edmund and
Leoba's shoulders and turned them
roughly to face the shore. "This is Hedeby.
It is a town of a thousand people! Look!"

Despite the fear that was turning his
knees to jelly, Edmund could not help
himself staring.

The huge boat was tied to a long wooden jetty that stretched back into the town and turned into a wooden road. On either side of this road there were hundreds of rectangular houses, each separated from its neighbour by a fence through which a gateway led up to a front door.

In the back yards, he could see chickens and pigs and children playing. A wide stream flowed through the middle of the town. Men led their horses over small bridges and women washed clothes at the water's edge.

But perhaps the strangest thing of all was the noise. Beside him Leoba stood in bewildered silence.

Men shouted. Horses whinnied. Women yelled. Animals squawked and squealed. There was the creak and rumble of cartwheels, the clash of metal and the steady pounding of hammer against wood.

Edmund turned to Captain Harald.

"What is to become of us?" he asked, desperately trying to keep a tremble out of his voice.

"You are to stay with Olaf and his kinsmen," replied Captain Harald. "They owe me a favour."

Before Edmund could speak again, the

red-bearded man stood up and sheathed his small dagger.

"Eat well with your hosts," he said. Then he turned on his heel and left them.

Leoba clutched her brother's arm. "Edmund!" she whispered. "What can this mean?"

At that moment, Olaf stepped forward and unlocked their chains. "Follow me," he said. "We go to the house of Guttorm and his wife Astrid."

Olaf jumped onto the wooden jetty and swung Edmund and Leoba down beside him.

"At least we are not chained anymore," whispered Leoba.

As she spoke, Edmund looked up at Olaf's face.

The big sailor looked out to sea and wouldn't meet his eyes.

4

Slaves For Sale

Leoba followed Edmund through the
crowded streets trying hard not to stare at
the men and women around her.

The women all wore a linen tunic with
a long sleeveless pinafore over the top.
Some pinafores were brown and some

were wonderful shades of blue. The huge
brooches fastening the shoulder straps
amazed Leoba.

There were always two of them linked
together with loops of silver chain or
beads. From the right hand brooch hung
keys, knives, needles and sometimes
scissors and a purse.

Olaf turned and smiled
at the look of astonishment
on her face. He pointed
to his own cloak
that was
pinned high
on his right
shoulder with
a massive
single brooch.

"See," he said, reaching with his right
hand across his body to the sheath of his

sword hanging on his left side. "We Vikings always keep our sword arm free."

For the first time Leoba spoke to Olaf. "Where do your brooches come from?" she asked.

Her voice was sweet and high and Edmund saw a look of tenderness pass over Olaf's face. He wondered if the Viking had children of his own.

"We make them ourselves," replied Olaf, proudly.

"One day I shall wear a brooch as fine as these," cried Leoba. Then she stopped and blushed, startled at the words that had rushed from her mouth.

Then Olaf turned abruptly down a side street and in at the first gateway on the left.

A wooden door opened in front of them and a small blonde-haired boy

peered round the edge.

"Halfdan!" cried
Olaf with a big smile.
"Have you forgotten
your Uncle Olaf already?"

The little boy shouted
and ran down the steps.
The noise brought a tall
pink-cheeked woman
to the door.

Her pretty face went
serious when she saw
Edmund and Leoba.
"Are these the children
sent by Harald the sea
captain?" she asked quietly.

Olaf nodded.

Astrid smiled at Edmund and Leoba. "You are welcome in our house," she said. "Come, and I will see to your needs."

"See!" whispered Leoba. "I *knew* something would go right for us!"

Edmund tried to reply but couldn't. He dropped behind and followed his sister through the door and into a room with a

packed earth floor.

In the middle of the house was the hearth room with two seating platforms on either side. A heavy iron cauldron hung from the ceiling over a pile of hot embers. The smell of new baked bread filled the air.

Leoba was entranced.

Astrid dipped a ladle in the steaming cauldron and filled two wooden bowls. "This is a stew of mutton and onions and cabbage, I hope you will like it."

"Shall I fetch a warm loaf from the oven, mother," said Halfdan in a high squeaky voice.

"Fetch two," said Astrid, kindly. Edmund looked into her wide honest face. Perhaps at last, he would learn the truth from this woman.

"How long do we stay with you?"
he asked.

At that moment
a man walked into
the room. He looked
just like Olaf except
he was shorter with
strongly muscled arms.
"I am Guttorm,"
he said. "You will
stay with us
for three days."

"The big market
is in three days,"
cried Halfdan,
clapping his hands.
"Father is buying
me a leather purse."
He turned to
Edmund and Leoba.

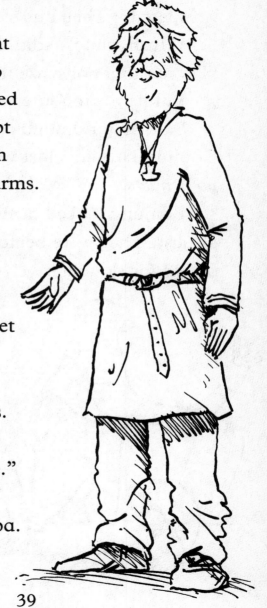

"Strange men come from the south," he whispered. "They buy slaves."

"Hush, child!" said Guttorm angrily. "Do not talk nonsense to our guests."

But it was too late.

Suddenly Edmund remembered Captain Harald's last words. *Eat well with your hosts.*

Edmund looked at the bowl of stew in disgust. They were being fattened like piglets for slaughter.

Beside him Leoba dropped the spoon that was halfway to her mouth and threw down her bowl. "I would rather starve than be a slave!" she screamed. Then she threw her arms around Edmund's shoulders and sobbed.

Edmund summoned all the strength he had left. "Half a moon ago, our parents were drowned," he said in a voice breaking with anger. "What kind of cruel people are you that would sell two orphans into slavery?"

Guttorm's face went white. "Your parents drowned half a moon ago?" he stammered.

Astrid breathed in sharply and clutched the amulet she wore around her neck.

Then she and Guttorm exchanged a long meaningful look.

"What is going on here?" demanded Olaf, banging his fist on the table.

"This is a matter for the gods," muttered Astrid. She went over to Leoba

and put her hands on her shoulders.
"Come with me, children. And do not be
afraid for now."

Something in her voice gave Edmund
and Leoba comfort. They let themselves
be led out of the house to the storeroom.

"Wait here and sleep," said Astrid.
She pulled out the two warm loaves.

Then she took the small amulet from around her neck and put it around Leoba's. "May the goddess Freya protect you both."

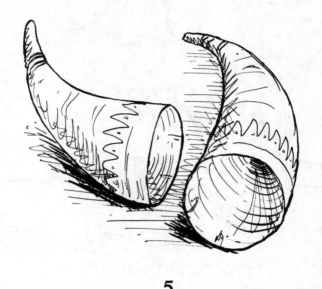

5

A Soothsayer's Prophecy

Guttorm poured out two horns of ale and sat down heavily beside his brother.

"You have bad news," said Olaf.

Guttorm nodded, drained his horn and filled it. For a moment he looked as if he didn't know where to begin.

"How long have you been gone from your home, Olaf?" he asked.

"A moon and more," replied Olaf. "Why do you ask?"

Guttorm took a deep breath. "Half a moon ago, Eric and Gudrun drowned. They were climbing the river gorge looking for blueberries. They slipped and fell."

Olaf stared but said nothing. Eric and Gudrun were his only children. Eric was just thirteen, Gudrun would have been eleven her next birthday.

"Your wife Kristin went to a soothsayer," continued Guttorm in a leaden voice. "The soothsayer told her she would bear no more children."

Olaf's shoulders slumped. He drained his horn of ale.

In the corner Astrid looked up. "The soothsayer gave Kristin some comfort," she said. "She promised you would have heirs. She said they would come from over the water. She said they would be a boy and a girl."

"It is a prophecy from the gods," said Guttorm, quietly.

"It is a gift," added Astrid.

The room was silent as the three adults

all thought the same thing.

Edmund and Leoba. Eric and Gudrun.

"Many of our kinsmen adopt, brother," said Guttorm, steadily. "It is a good and honourable tradition."

Olaf rubbed a heavy hand over his face. "I know, I know," he said in a low voice. "Perhaps I have known something of this all along." He paused and his horn trembled in his hand. "Even during the sea journey, I found myself growing fond of these children. They are brave and loyal to each other."

He looked up and his face was full of anguish. "But what can I do? Even if they agree to come with me, and I am no kidnapper," he added fiercely, "I have given my word to Harald the sea captain."

Olaf sighed heavily. "Harald is a cruel and greedy man."

"It is *I* who owes him the favour," said Guttorm in a firm voice. "And a gift from the gods cannot be ignored."

Guttorm drained his horn of ale. "Besides Harald only wants silver. I will pay him his silver."

Olaf looked up, astonished. "But how can I pay you? I have no silver."

"You are my only brother," said Guttorm, slowly. "That is silver enough for me."

❖

Edmund was in the middle of a dream.
He was working on a farm. The sheds had
low thick walls and the
roofs were covered in turf.
On the top of one shed,
two goats were nibbling
the shiny green grass.

Suddenly, Edmund
woke and opened
his eyes.

Olaf was
standing by the
storeroom door.

Edmund felt his
belly tighten but he
didn't feel afraid.
"Olaf," he whispered.

Olaf turned and sat down beside him. "Wake your sister, Edmund," he said. "I have something to tell you and I want you to tell me something, too."

6

A Dream Come True

Olaf, Edmund and Leoba sat in silence in the dark early morning.

Under their rough blanket, Edmund and Leoba held hands, trying to take in all that Olaf had told them.

They would have a new life with him

and his wife. Edmund would help Olaf farm his land. Leoba would learn the skills of a Viking woman. But they had to come of their own free will.

"For I would not take you against your will," said Olaf.

"We shall never see our home again, shall we?" said Leoba. Even though she knew now this was so, she wanted someone to say it out loud.

"No," said Olaf. "You will make a new home with me."

"Does Captain Harald plan to sell us as slaves?" asked Edmund.

"Most certainly," said Olaf. "Many slaves are captured each year and sold in the market." He paused. "You would have made him a great deal of silver."

Leoba shuddered. "What happens to them?" she asked in a choked voice.

"Many are forced into labour for the
rest of their lives. Some, especially young
ones are taken south by the Arab traders,"
Olaf shook his head. "None are ever heard
of again."

Suddenly the door swung open and
Astrid ran into the room.

"You must leave," she cried. "Captain Harald has heard of your news, Olaf, and he has guessed your mind. He will not accept silver from Guttorm."

Olaf leapt to his feet. "What will you do?"

"Harald also wants axe heads from Guttorm," replied Astrid quickly. "A deal will be struck." Her eyes flashed. "You must go!"

Olaf turned to Edmund and Leoba. "Do you come willingly?"

"Yes."

Olaf's teeth shone in the moonlight. For a second his large hands rested lightly on their heads.

56

"Good. We leave now."

Astrid pushed a bag at them. "Here is food. There is a boat on the stream. My brother's ship waits for you in the harbour."

She touched Edmund and Leoba's shoulders. "May the gods protect you."

"Your amulet!" cried Leoba. She began to pull it over her head.

"Keep it," said Astrid. She squeezed Leoba's arm. "A present from your new kinswoman."

Leoba felt her throat tighten with tears. She had not known such kindness

since her own mother had died.

The next minute Edmund and Leoba
were on their hands and knees following
Olaf through the long grass down to the
edge of the stream.

Edmund stared in amazement as he
stood beside Olaf on the brow of a hill.

A farm nestled in a valley below them.

Beyond it was lake of glassy black water. Around the main farmhouse several small sheds were scattered. They had thick low walls and the roofs were covered in turf.

On one shed two goats were tethered. Edmund gasped.

"What is it?" asked Olaf. "Is something wrong? We are home. This is my farm."

For a moment Edmund could barely speak. "It – it," he stammered. "It is the farm I was dreaming of when you came to us that night. The night we escaped from Hedeby."

Olaf put his hand on Edmund's shoulder. "I am glad," he said. "The soothsayer was right. Perhaps now we can put behind us all the terrible things that have happened and start a new life together."

At that moment
Leoba joined them. She wore
a circle of flowers in her hair and
her skirt was bulging with berries.

"Look!" she cried, pointing down the
hill and waving. "Who's that?"

A young woman with a bright red head-
scarf stood in front of the farmhouse

A broad smile crossed Olaf's face.

"That's Kristin," he cried. "She is waiting
for us!" He cupped his hands around his
mouth. "Kristin!"

Then he took Edmund and Leoba by
the hand and began to walk quickly down
the hill.

Notes

Viking Raids

Vikings from Norway and Denmark began raiding the British Isles towards the end of the eighth century. The raids began as a way of re-stocking ships with meat and vegetables and turned into wholesale looting of valuables and the capture of slaves for sale in trading towns like Hedeby. Many Viking raiders were part-time farmers.

Viking Ships

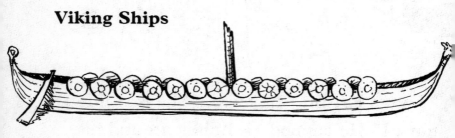

Vikings used two kinds of ships – long ships which were fast and easy to manoeuvre and trading ships which were slow and broader. In good winds a long ship could sail at seven knots. If the wind dropped the sailors rowed. Both types of ship had flattish

bottoms and shallow drafts which meant they
could go up rivers or be dragged onto beaches.

Hedeby

Hedeby was a town of craftsmen and traders on
the Jutland Peninsula where the trade routes
between the North Sea, the Baltic Sea and Western
Europe came together. From the south came glass,
wine, silk, sword blades and jewellery. From the
north came furs, ivory, iron, rope and slaves
captured on raiding parties. Farmers sold butter,
cheese and grain.

Sparks: Historical Adventures

ANCIENT GREECE
The Great Horse of Troy – The Trojan War
0 7496 3369 7 (hbk)   0 7496 3538 X (pbk)
The Winner's Wreath – Ancient Greek Olympics
0 7496 3368 9 (hbk)   0 7496 3555 X (pbk)

INVADERS AND SETTLERS
Boudicca Strikes Back – The Romans in Britain
0 7496 3366 2 (hbk)   0 7496 3546 0 (pbk)
Viking Raiders – A Norse Attack
0 7496 3089 2 (hbk)   0 7496 3457 X (pbk)
Erik's New Home – A Viking Town
0 7496 3367 0 (hbk)   0 7496 3552 5 (pbk)

TALES OF THE ROWDY ROMANS
The Great Necklace Hunt
0 7496 2221 0 (hbk)   0 7496 2628 3 (pbk)
The Lost Legionary
0 7496 2222 9 (hbk)   0 7496 2629 1 (pbk)
The Guard Dog Geese
0 7496 2331 4 (hbk)   0 7496 2630 5 (pbk)
A Runaway Donkey
0 7496 2332 2 (hbk)   0 7496 2631 3 (pbk)

TUDORS AND STUARTS
Captain Drake's Orders – The Armada
0 7496 2556 2 (hbk)   0 7496 3121 X (pbk)
London's Burning – The Great Fire of London
0 7496 2557 0 (hbk)   0 7496 3122 8 (pbk)
Mystery at the Globe – Shakespeare's Theatre
0 7496 3096 5 (hbk)   0 7496 3449 9 (pbk)
Plague! – A Tudor Epidemic
0 7496 3365 4 (hbk)   0 7496 3556 8 (pbk)
Stranger in the Glen – Rob Roy
0 7496 2586 4 (hbk)   0 7496 3123 6 (pbk)
A Dream of Danger – The Massacre of Glencoe
0 7496 2587 2 (hbk)   0 7496 3124 4 (pbk)
A Queen's Promise – Mary Queen of Scots
0 7496 2589 9 (hbk)   0 7496 3125 2 (pbk)
Over the Sea to Skye – Bonnie Prince Charlie
0 7496 2588 0 (hbk)   0 7496 3126 0 (pbk)

TALES OF A TUDOR TEARAWAY
A Pig Called Henry
0 7496 2204 4 (hbk)   0 7496 2625 9 (pbk)
A Horse Called Deathblow
0 7496 2205 9 (hbk)   0 7496 2624 0 (pbk)
Dancing for Captain Drake
0 7496 2234 2 (hbk)   0 7496 2626 7 (pbk)
Birthdays are a Serious Business
0 7496 2235 0 (hbk)   0 7496 2627 5 (pbk)

VICTORIAN ERA
The Runaway Slave – The British Slave Trade
0 7496 3093 0 (hbk)   0 7496 3456 1 (pbk)
The Sewer Sleuth – Victorian Cholera
0 7496 2590 2 (hbk)   0 7496 3128 7 (pbk)
Convict! – Criminals Sent to Australia
0 7496 2591 0 (hbk)   0 7496 3129 5 (pbk)
An Indian Adventure – Victorian India
0 7496 3090 6 (hbk)   0 7496 3451 0 (pbk)
Farewell to Ireland – Emigration to America
0 7496 3094 9 (hbk)   0 7496 3448 0 (pbk)
The Great Hunger – Famine in Ireland
0 7496 3095 7 (hbk)   0 7496 3447 2 (pbk)
Fire Down the Pit – A Welsh Mining Disaster
0 7496 3091 4 (hbk)   0 7496 3450 2 (pbk)
Tunnel Rescue – The Great Western Railway
0 7496 3353 0 (hbk)   0 7496 3537 1 (pbk)
Kidnap on the Canal – Victorian Waterways
0 7496 3352 2 (hbk)   0 7496 3540 1 (pbk)
Dr. Barnardo's Boys – Victorian Charity
0 7496 3358 1 (hbk)   0 7496 3541 X (pbk)
The Iron Ship – Brunel's Great Britain
0 7496 3355 7 (hbk)   0 7496 3543 6 (pbk)
Bodies for Sale – Victorian Tomb-Robbers
0 7496 3364 6 (hbk)   0 7496 3539 8 (pbk)
Penny Post Boy – The Victorian Postal Service
0 7496 3362 X (hbk)   0 7496 3544 4 (pbk)
The Canal Diggers – The Manchester Ship Canal
0 7496 3356 5 (hbk)   0 7496 3545 2 (pbk)
The Tay Bridge Tragedy – A Victorian Disaster
0 7496 3354 9 (hbk)   0 7496 3547 9 (pbk)
Stop, Thief! – The Victorian Police
0 7496 3359 X (hbk)   0 7496 3548 7 (pbk)
Miss Buss and Miss Beale – Victorian Schools
0 7496 3360 3 (hbk)   0 7496 3549 5 (pbk)
Chimney Charlie – Victorian Chimney Sweeps
0 7496 3351 4 (hbk)   0 7496 3551 7 (pbk)
Down the Drain – Victorian Sewers
0 7496 3357 3 (hbk)   0 7496 3550 9 (pbk)
The Ideal Home – A Victorian New Town
0 7496 3361 1 (hbk)   0 7496 3553 3 (pbk)
Stage Struck – Victorian Music Hall
0 7496 3367 0 (hbk)   0 7496 3554 1 (pbk)

TRAVELS OF A YOUNG VICTORIAN
The Golden Key
0 7496 2360 8 (hbk)   0 7496 2632 1 (pbk)
Poppy's Big Push
0 7496 2361 6 (hbk)   0 7496 2633 X (pbk)
Poppy's Secret
0 7496 2374 8 (hbk)   0 7496 2634 8 (pbk)
The Lost Treasure
0 7496 2375 6 (hbk)   0 7496 2635 6 (pbk)

20th-CENTURY HISTORY
Fight for the Vote – The Suffragettes
0 7496 3092 2 (hbk)   0 7496 3452 9 (pbk)
The Road to London – The Jarrow March
0 7496 2609 7 (hbk)   0 7496 3132 5 (pbk)
The Sandbag Secret – The Blitz
0 7496 2608 9 (hbk)   0 7496 3133 3 (pbk)
Sid's War – Evacuation
0 7496 3209 7 (hbk)   0 7496 3445 6 (pbk)
D-Day! – Wartime Adventure
0 7496 3208 9 (hbk)   0 7496 3446 4 (pbk)
The Prisoner – A Prisoner of War
0 7496 3212 7 (hbk)   0 7496 3455 3 (pbk)
Escape from Germany – Wartime Refugees
0 7496 3211 9 (hbk)   0 7496 3454 5 (pbk)
Flying Bombs – Wartime Bomb Disposal
0 7496 3210 0 (hbk)   0 7496 3453 7 (pbk)
12,000 Miles From Home – Sent to Australia
0 7496 3370 0 (hbk)   0 7496 3542 8 (pbk)